Chrissy Banks

The Uninvited

Indigo Dreams Publishing

First Edition: The Uninvited
First published in Great Britain in 2019 by:
Indigo Dreams Publishing
24, Forest Houses
Cookworthy Moor
Halwill
Beaworthy
Devon
EX21 5UU

www.indigodreams.co.uk

Chrissy Banks has asserted her right under the Copyright, Designs and Patents Act 1988 to be identified as the author of this work.

ISBN 978-1-912876-13-6

British Library Cataloguing in Publication Data. A CIP record for this book can be obtained from the British Library.

Designed and typeset in Palatino Linotype by Indigo Dreams.
Cover design by Ronnie Goodyer at Indigo Dreams
Printed and bound in Great Britain by 4edge Ltd.

Papers used by Indigo Dreams are recyclable products made from wood grown in sustainable forests following the guidance of the Forest Stewardship Council.

for the Lost

Acknowledgments

Thanks to all those writers, editors, friends and family members who have supported, challenged and encouraged me over the years, especially Sue Boyle and Bath Cafe Writers, Fire River Poets, Mincing Poets, Secret Poets, Somerset Writers and We 3. A big thank you also to Ronnie and Dawn at Indigo Dreams for selecting this collection for publication.

Versions of some of these poems have appeared in the following magazines and anthologies:

Reach Poetry, And Other Poems, Envoi, Clear Poetry, the Rialto, the Lake, South, Antiphon, Orbis, Ware Poets Competition Anthology, the Journal, Ink Sweat & Tears, Battered Moons Competition Anthology, Obsessed with Pipework, Smiths Knoll, the Broadsheet, Frogmore Papers, Weyfarers.

Also by Chrissy Banks:

Days of Fire and Flood, original plus, 2005.
Watching the Home Movies, Odyssey Press, 1996.

CONTENTS

The Uninvited 9

Rhubarb and Kippers 10

When We Were Manx 11

The Gooseneck, Ballabrooie 12

November 22nd, 1963.. 13

The Horrible Haircuts of Childhood................................ 14

The Tale of the Cake 15

Things My Mother Said 17

Mrs Belmain at Number One 18

Remembering Uncle Lawrence... 19

All Those Parties 20

The Year of the Zebra 21

Addicted to Blue 22

en route with angels 23

Cliff Top 24

Finn... 25

Sleeper 26

Constantin... 27

The Secret Bees 28

The Word 29

The Neighbour 30

A Serious Word.. 31

How do you know it's an emergency? 33

In the Middle of the Night I Look For Reasons 35

Lost 37

If you don't come back... 38

Your Story... 39

The Death of Li Po 40

Survival 41

The Weather In Your Absence 42

Spilt 43

Scene on a Hotel Balcony 45

Forty Years 46

Poem Withot 47

You Have Reached Your Destination.. 48

The Key.. 49

Found... 50

Practising Presence 51

Acceptance 52

Ploubalay... 53

Rio, Summer 2014 54

Mrs Blake Helps Out 55

Lilies White Heaven.. 56

Iris I 57

Iris II... 58

Penny Whistle... 58

The Touch.. 60

The Sex Life of Paper Clips 62

In Need of Some Attention 63

The Babysitter Goes Ballroom 64

After Captain Underpants, the Big Question 65

An Agnostic's Christmas 66

Ferry Across New Year 67

Washing the Buddha 68

The Uninvited

The Uninvited

We flew to a country of golden temples,
golden Buddhas six times as tall as a man.
But now, here's what I think about most:

Garden lodge. Petal-strewn bed. Bowl of fruit
on a table. Banana skin partially stripped, flesh
well chomped, not by us. Too munched for a mouse.

I ransacked cupboards, peered under chairs.
Searched for a hole, a gap, a crack big enough.
Had I left a window open, a door unlatched?

Someone delivered a metal cage, banana-baited.
At first, not a squeak. Then I woke to a maniac
rattling of bars. The thing and I stared at each other.

Fingery claws, breathing fur. The naked flex
of its tail; those eyes, onyx-black. I could just about watch
as it shivered there in the cage. But when it was gone,

it was still here. In a sealed wooden house.
Me and the creature: all one, according to Buddha.
What lives in shadow is always seeking a gap.

Rhubarb and Kippers
after Jo Roach

I come from Quinns and Foxes, from women
whose eyes were drills, who spoke in proverbs,
bright-lipped women, who laughed till they wept;
from men in jackets with sagging pockets,
smelling of sweat and tobacco, menders of things,
men who shouted at football on television.

I come from a vacant front room, a stink
of paraffin; from tea cosies, hairnets and rollers.
I come from gossip and what Jesus said,
best clothes on the sabbath, prayers before bed,
fish on Friday, a Sunday roast; walnut whips,
Bunty and Jackie, Green Goddess shampoo,
hydrangeas and roses, a rhubarb patch.

I come from the Beatles and Stones, the two
Dylans, from Monty Python and the crushing foot.
I come from heather and gorse, hills and glens;
from ferry boats, B&Bs on the curving prom.
I come from the lighthouse, from gulls and grey seas.
I come from the animal howl of the foghorn,
my eyes fixed on the horizon till the day I left.

When We Were Manx

Manx meant we had sea in our veins
and the blood of Celts; or Vikings
who rowed to the island in dragonhead boats.
The sea fed us, kipper and mackerel common as cake.
Our songs were of wrecked ships, our stories
of ghosts in the castle, fairies under the bridge.
In our throats, salt, mountain air, the hit
of burnt rubber and petrol fumes
from the throttles of revving bikes.

In our teens, we took holiday work
in the rock factory shop.
The stuff emerged first in a long roll of flamingo.
We aproned up and pushed it backwards and forwards
into a six foot coil.
Tourists watched, glad to be out of the rain.
We cut the rock in regular lengths
and after it hardened, packed it away
in a metal box, heaved it along to the store room
fending off Kevin, who'd corner us if he could.

The older girls were mainly comeovers
from across. Fairy light towns threaded horizons
called us away to the scattered places we inhabit now.

That sticky-skinned stuff: a three legs of man,
like a vein or a core, ran right through (still does)
the bite white centre,
from left to right, bottom to top.

The Gooseneck, Ballabrooie

this way   through the gap in the hedge
        climb into a country that jumps and crawls
            a place to scramble through grass and tall ferns
                to trail along ditches & mud paths

we like to stroke minky caterpillars
        & make grasshoppers jump but parson's pigs
        are boring grey like we must be at school
                clean   combed   and stuffed into a uniform

wading through brambles our skin rips
        arms piled chin-high with branches
        scaffolding for the den we'll build
                our pockets alive with snails to race

time is slow   the future only as far as tomorrow
        how can we know that growing up
        will make us exiles new kids replacing us
                new needs pulling us far

from the grasslands   the fringes of hawthorn and elder
        further from careless play
        the day so close when all this wild
                will choke under a hundred houses

parson's pig – a Manx term for a woodlouse

November 22nd, 1963

Already that morning, I'd glared three times
in the charm-free mirror that hung skew-whiff
over the mantelpiece. Chicken pox
had made a Jackson Pollack of my face.
Soon my skin would be all scratched off.
No school. The finger of exile had pointed
to our back room, where the telly jabbered away.

Meanwhile, rumours of simmering stew
leaked from the kitchen, my mother
on percussive saucepans behind again,
clanging. The coal fire shiffled and ticked.

A car in Dallas sleeks across the screen,
Jackie with Black Magic hair, an ice cream smile,
her husband polished to a sheen. Crinkly eyes.
The crowd goes mental as they pass.
But now what's going on? A cameraman
lurches. The president's slumped in his wife's
blood-mottled lap as she begs us to look away.

Cradling a new-born tragedy
to lay in my mother's arms,
I fly to the kitchen. But the death
of the just-bloomed President of the USA
is not enough to break the martyr's long watch
at the altar of the oven. Not enough
to change again the interrupted features of her *whatnow* face.

I could feel it then, a new skin forming,
tight enough to hold my own ramshackle self,
but soft and permeable like bandage,
so that the world could come bleeding through.

The Horrible Haircuts of Childhood

I remember the horrible haircuts:
trapped in the chair, tied up in a nylon gown,
condemned to watching it happen, mute,
full-face in the mirror. Like viewing your own
execution, while the Serial Hair Killer witters
about holidays, shopping, school, the weather,
pretending there's no ritual sacrifice going on
as she shreds you with eager scissors.

My hair was never that long in the first place
and the short, blunt cut was always wrong,
the way a pair of curtains, hung,
but chopped in half, are wrong. My face,
stripped naked, too plainly showed I longed
to die quickly, all hiding places gone.

the tale of the cake

in our house
it was always my mother
giving an order
wagging a finger
the one to deliver
news of a rumour
of shocking behaviour –
me or my brother –
sending her into a lather
& offending apparently
both earthly and heavenly father

so i loved when she'd tell
the tale of the cake
how the aroma of chocolate
and warm caramel
took her under its spell
as she lifted
the sponge she'd baked
from the oven

and it fell from her grip
scattering pieces pell mell
all over the sticky tiled floor

their faces contorted in horror
my mother and father stare
at the chocolatey lure
aching with cake lust
they drop
to the floor
scoop
to their tingling lips

handfuls of sponge
hot sweet and soft
do not stop
till they've polished it all off

Things My Mother Said

She said *I've got eyes in the back of my head*
        I just don't understand you she said
        you should be ashamed of yourself
She said *Look what you've made me do now.*
When I asked how old she was she said
        As old as my gums and a little bit older than my teeth
She said *Don't let anyone see you down there*
        Men! she said *Men!*

When I was a teenager she looked me up and down
and said *That dress does nothing for you*
But sometimes she said *Go and enjoy yourself love*
and when I came back *Who did you meet?*
Whoever it was she knew their family history
She often asked me *What's the skeet?*
but I had none and if I had
I wouldn't have given it to her.

She always had her sights on the weather
        You're not going out without a coat in this
        It's fit to blow your head off
Sometimes she'd look me in the eye and say
        Bless you love bless you, meaning *thank you*
        meaning *I love you.*

She said *I'll never make old bones*
When her hearing went she said
        Speak up you're mumbling
she said *It's no joke getting old*
In her last year she said
        86! Would you believe it?

skeet – a Manx word meaning gossip

Mrs Belmain at Number One

The word *chignon* could have been coined
for the sweep of her hair, the word *svelte*
for her shins. The words *chic* and *allure* shone
all over her Catherine Deneuve demeanour.
She lived in the red-brick semi-detached at the top,
with Gill, her round-shouldered daughter.

Smart, bonny, presentable. None of the mothers'
usual words would do. Who else stepped out
in stilettos, tapping a black umbrella with pointed tip?
Who else angled her chin at a regal tilt, shoulders back,
spine straight as a model for Yves St Laurent?
The mothers stared whenever she strode out.
The phrase *Who does she think she is?* sprang
from their lips, the word *snob,* the word *slut.*

Remembering Uncle Lawrence

Two memories of Uncle Lawrence, brother
to neither my father nor mother, survive.
In the first he is plucking a goose – his deft tugs
loose the quills; little raised pocks in the yellow flesh.

Second, I'm aged seven or so; the family is leaving
the island at night on a ferry boat. Uncle Lawrence
brings me a scratchy blanket, strokes my hair.
Who was Uncle Lawrence and why was he there?

All Those Parties

Someone trod smoky bacon crisps
and chocolate cake into the pink nylon carpet
and someone helped themselves
to all the bottles in her father's booze cupboard,
drained them dry and lurched out
into the garden for a piss, threw empties
all over the lawn and into the pond
where the gnomes were poised for fishing.
And someone went upstairs
with someone else's girlfriend
and wrestled with her
all over the gold parental candlewick,
but the boyfriend crashed through the door
and thumped the kid and thumped him again
till his nose bloodied the polycotton easycare sheets
and the girl screamed and ran downstairs
in daisy-patterned knickers and a flood of tears.
And close to midnight someone said, *Who's that?*
and the party girl's parents marched in,
her mother speechless, her father barking,
God in heaven, what's been happening here?!

Or so someone told me later.
I was stretched out on the chintz three-seater,
liplocked to John the One –

till the door flew wide,
all the lights in the room glared down
and *A Groovy Kind of Love*
scraped to a halt.

The Year of the Zebra

It was the year the spinning-top world
was a-wobble, money dissolving like chocolate
in the sun. The year they scuppered our jobs.
Faultlines cracked, ground collapsed.

Evenings, starlings printed the heavens –
deleted their text in swerving reverse.
It was the year death snatched a friend,
hammered her heart till it stopped.

The year of underground ruptures, a flood,
foot and mouth, bombings and blood.
And Canterbury sun spliced cathedral windows,
a zebra strolled out of the shadows.

Closer to home, the newly-weds crashed
to earth, a black box ending to love.
And we walked so far there was no turning back.
Dark came down, a furious storm blew up.

I thought we were lost, but a hand reached
for mine, gleam of lights in the distance.
Inside, a fire, food and drink at the inn.
The year of a birth, warmth in my arms again.

Addicted to Blue

Sometimes a feeling sits by your side,
places a muzzle in your lap and sighs.
Even a feeling that drools and rolls
its pitiful eyes at you, becomes a friend.

Mine was called Blue. I sat in the dark,
stroking the slobbering beast, read Hardy
and Sylvia Plath. Played Hendrix and Bob
on a loop. I was drinking too much.

But the sight of the purple haze when I walked
in the bluebell fields was a different drug.
Hooked, I went back day after day. Returned
the following year with a different dog.

en route with angels

       batting down the motorway
in darkening rain, wipers slicing vision,
no doubt headed for a jam, a pile-up.

       but angels are singing on the radio,
ice-sharp, sky-climbing notes that arch and
overchime each other in a peal of light.

       an angel therapist reveals how
she employs these holy helpers, insists
our own angelic guides exist.

       an angeloligist draws their flight-path
round her chandelier, names each one.
and now, if mine is out there somewhere, come.

       it fills the windscreen in a sudden flap
of crow, thrown and spread as though suspended
on a cross, head-on, black eyes piercing me.

       there and gone, a millisecond from collision.
come on, it's just a kamikaze crow -
but i'm slowing, looking for an exit.

Cliff Top

a bliss-blue sea and sky
flourish of whipped cream clouds
buttercup fields daygloed
in green and gold

all swim to a blur
as our focus turns

      to this dandelion clock
      seedbomb that ticks
      in the foreground

Finn

I'm stopped
       by your lovely wild face
       looking out from a poster
       fixed to a gate

hey Finn
       there you are

the poster says
       you wear an ear-stretcher
I imagine you dancing
some Festival field
       your whisky-brown hair
       doing its own fling

hey Finn
       I wish I had seen you
       without the word *Missing*
       printed across your chest

Sleeper

The street outside is quiet as sixpence
        in a satin purse.

What month is this?
        I dreamed I was awake.
And now the sounds
        of nobody, a silent phone.
The mirror tells
        my hair's grown long and grey.

Where are my children?
        Will they be waiting for me
still at school, grown too big
        for their uniforms?
Orphans. Who will have loved them
        if it wasn't me?

I've slept so long –
        while pansies dared to push
their purple faces into sullen air
        while fledgling sparrows flew.

Constantin

I knew a man, young and gently spoken,
who couldn't leave home. His eyes were soft,
he was easy to love. You could see how
he'd shift like dry sand to make a place for another,
but underneath was rock, where his soul crouched,
hidden. His father lived in a wheelchair. He was fading,
but loved a joke. The son imagined
carrying his father's coffin into the church.
When he looked at his mother, he couldn't get free
of her eyes. He asked me, 'Why is it so often
I think of a cello? I feel like the inside of a cello
without a bow?' He asked me as if I would know
and I thought, *If I could set him vibrating* –
I noticed the sheen on his cheek, on his arms
where they were deepest brown.
He came to me on those dim, grey afternoons
and it gave comfort to us both,
but I would never be the bow.

The Secret Bees

This young girl with closed lips,
 eyes too big for her face, pale eyes
that look straight through a man –
hidden under her coat, she wears

a dress of bees. Electric, they hover
over her skin, or squat on her flesh,
nosing and nudging, a swarm
that bustles and nuzzles and stings.

Something happened to let them in.
The bees have made her theirs alone.
She will not tell anyone.

The Word

She dreamt she was ripping butterfly wings, tearing apart the gorgeous purple and red, thin as a petal of silk dipped in ink, wings still twitching that peeled apart as she pulled. And she woke with the parasite guilt in her gut, where it would feast, where it would banquet, while she starved. And it was the Word.

The Word saw need and throttled it, till it was a whimper in a dusty corner and the Word demanded thirty pounds of flesh for its release.

She wanted to be soul, not body, hated living in her skin, having to eat, drink, go naked; and the mirrored twin, her mutinous body, thief of childhood, she wanted it timelocked and sapling thin. And all that stuff her body lately, her fleshy body, hungered for: her lips, thighs open to another. Traitor body, her body breaking, bursting, her bully mind turning on her body, giving in.

But sometimes, a creature newly formed began to lift one wing, then the other, opening its red and purple to the warming day, imagining the succulence of lilac, zinnias.

The Neighbour

Sometimes I thought I'd call,
invite her in. *Hi. I'm from next door.*
If there's anything we can do.....
Good intentions, nothing more.

Mostly, I hardly thought of her at all.
The few times I saw her out,
she didn't speak, head down, wrapped
in a scarf, her steps quick, small.

Her blinds are closed today,
but then they almost always are.
I 'd no idea how she spent her time
or who were the bearded men I saw

pull up in a big-booted car, a solemn
deputation, who would disappear
into her house, their wired expressions
forbidding any wish of mine to stare.

Yesterday the police rapped on my door,
asking questions. Then the press came.
Until you mentioned it, I said,
I didn't even know her name.

A Serious Word

I couldn't find the key anywhere,
so I'm thinking maybe I've thrown it out
accidentally in the rubbish
and I'm rummaging through the gloop
from five days' meals – beer cans
and a mountain of soggy tissues from a cold
I couldn't throw off – when my hand
comes up against something
hard and smooth that I can feel the metal weight of
as I draw it up through the gunk,
but not till I'm wiping off carrot peel and gravy
do I finally see I'm holding a fucking gun.
I mean, can you believe it?
And I'm standing there,
wondering what to do with it,
when Tron, you know my son Tron,
marches into the kitchen
and seeing the thing in my hand
goes for me as though I've stolen it from him,
or like I've totally shot his plan
to do away with his teacher and all of his class.
So I ask him where it comes from
and he tells me school
and I'm thinking what kind of school lends *firearms*
to thirteen year old kids?
But Tron has grabbed the gun
and he's pointing it at me.
Can you imagine, I'm screaming my fucking head off.
And although as it happens it isn't *his* gun
and as it turns out, it isn't actually a gun, a real gun,
even so it gets me thinking
how kind of unusual he is, Tron,
anti-social even, and you know,

I'm wondering if I might not have to
get his big sister to have a serious word,
in case he goes and does something
we might not live to regret.

How do you know it's an emergency?

fever cold nausea a rash
shortness-of-breath

How do you know it's an emergency?
the doctors are on sick leave
your op's rescheduled once again

How do you know it's an emergency?
the sleeping bags in doorways
the queues for food   lately not even a dog

How do you know it's an emergency?
they cut the fat   they cut the flesh
and now they cut the vein

How do you know it's an emergency?
a stampede a stampede
a man with two guns and a butcher's knife

How do you know it's an emergency?
the charred skeletons of buildings
the charred skeletons

How do you know it's an emergency?
the sea is in the streets
the chairs and tables are swimming

How do you know it's an emergency?
as water rises crew and captain
avoid counting the lifeboats

How do you know it's an emergency?
as we sail towards the waterfall
crew and captain look the other way

How do you know it's an emergency?
they could still turn around
they will not turn around

How do you know it's an emergency?
fever cold nausea a rash
shortness   of breath

In the Middle of the Night I Look For Reasons
(November 2016)

Maybe it was the rain that day or the letter in the post
or the door let go in your face or the way the rubbish
was strewn all over the place outside your house.
Maybe it was the delivery man's indecipherable phrase.
Maybe it was something about the knowledge of how little
you realised you'd been able to save.

Maybe it was an unspoken family pact. You and
those with your family name, back, back, back,
through the generations, just what you'd always done.
Maybe you were nostalgic for your father, who talked tough,
who stood, fists up, between you and the bear.
Maybe you thought of your mother,
who spoiled whatever you treasured
and told you off in a spotless room with a quiet lock.
Or did you recall a land of tea and ginger cake
where your grandparents snuggled up,
their wifiless world of christenings and small-town shocks?

Maybe you closed your eyes and let chance make its mark.
Or you thought the whole malarkey was fixed by God or Fate
or planetary alignments so there could only be one result.
Maybe you imagined yours wasn't even a speaking part,
your silent shout wouldn't count.

Maybe you wanted to say *I am different* or *I've had enough*
or *This has got to stop.* You longed to believe in a Messiah.
Maybe you wanted it like falling in love. Wanted it *so much*
you imagined your wanting could make it happen.

Maybe no-one could explain in a way
that didn't make you feel stupid.

And just when you thought you were clear
who you could or could not trust, the trees in the forest
all swapped places and you couldn't remember
which direction the sun was coming from.

Maybe there's no reason, or many, or one.

Lost

We have run through the city too fast.
We must wait for our souls to catch up.
We are searching, we fear they are lost.

We have grown unaccustomed to waiting.
We are restless as children in silence.
And how to be still without wanting?

All that we have is nothing. All that we know
is nothing. What must we do who rely on doing,
now we have only breathing, being and now?

We cannot be sure they will return at all,
our souls. Our hearts are hollowed-out bowls
we hold under a fevered sky for rain to fall.

We are lonely without ourselves and each other.
We call out all the names we know for our souls.
We call them again. We call them over and over.

If you don't come back

I will turn to the woods.
To winter woods
trees rising above
their heap of leaves.
I'll turn to the hills that endure
rain, flood, fog, snow and storm
the worst winds and fires of full sun.
I will follow the river that keeps on
flowing, keeps on carrying
pike and trout and stickleback
despite its sinkage of stones.
I'll turn to the garden
and watch how it dies
then grows; to the swift visits
of winking-winged brimstones
the patient journeys of ants.
And I will turn to the sea
the sea that will rumble me
slap me awake, holding
its mirror to my face.
I'll look to the waves' rise and fall
moon-pulled, thrown by wind
into foam. Even to the cold
deep places, where I can stand
alone, till I am blue boned.

Your Story
(i.m.Tony Charles)

I can hear you now
telling the story loving it
who passed to whom and how
who bottled it nutted it fumbled it
who bundled in and won the ball
the balletic footwork the swerves
the surge forward the offside call
the soaring arcs the angled curves
and the tackles that took the piss
the goal-kick you whacked
that hit-the-post near-miss
and the opposition gobsmacked
by this giant bald bloke (you)
careering down the left wing
like a rhino stampeding through
booting the ball straight in
– *yes!* – the leaps whoops fists
in the air you in the midst
of a scrum of adoring optimists

whistle blows and you're off again
second attempt at glory
and it comes after their number ten's
sliding tackle the fleeting furore
free throw to you possession is sweet
your magnificent run with the ball tame
as a well-trained pup at your feet
you're way out ahead in charge of the game
and no-one can touch you hold you stop you

but you're down smack headlong
nobody near and no-one felled you
pain in your heart a lifetime's cargo.

The Death of Li Po

He's ten parts love, ten parts
poetry. The rest is wine.

He's tried his words on the full moon,
but there's no wooing her.
She smiles, her cool beauty
exposed to every man.

Fool, he'll never possess her,
but a drunken romantic is doomed
to try to the end.

Tonight, he pushes his boat out on the river, reaches out
to stroke her face as it shimmers,
dodging his touch. Further and further he leans.

Face down in the water,
what use to him now are poetry and love?

But he expires, words on his tongue,
the moon in his arms.

Survival

Loping across the night lawn
to pick at remains of the funeral lunch

red as the falling leaves
nose sharp as an arrowhead

the beautiful hunted fox
the fox that can kill for no reason.

*

I still can't believe it
the widow says.

Death's landslide
has smothered their future.

His sons manage the event
in their different ways -

one slips back instantly
into the sheath of student life

one auditions for his father's part
repeats his sayings
with an over-exuberant laugh

and one alone at the window at night
watches the fox going about
its solitary work of survival

taking food into the wooded shadows
daring time and again
to come back into the light for more.

The Weather In Your Absence

Rain in July. Smoked sky arrows it down
to pelt the patio. I watch it rebound
in a hot-coals, jumping-jack dance
of splash and ripple, ripple and splash.

Air, rain, cloud: a summer of gunmetal grey.
And you, for weeks now, months, staying away.
Your voice, one of the rare times we speak,
is sharp as arched talons. The cold shock
again of finding that blackbird on its back,
in the front garden, red tear at its neck.

All day your absence, rain's pitiless patter.
I wish the sun would pour over it all litres
of warm light. *Summer never should be like this.*
No, says the rain. *But it is, it is, it is.*

Spilt

I was besotted. Twenty, but still a child,
clinging to a lifeboat made of poetry and love -
my skewed idea of it: linked hands, red
lipstick, a shallow dive into warm water.
I held my hopes carefully so they wouldn't spill,
feeding him thoughts taken from books and film.

We went to see *Don't Look Now,* a film
rippling with premonition. As a child,
I feared I could leak out and others spill
into me, mostly those who claimed love,
as if all my body was made of was water.
I was a little edgy too about the colour red.

This film was like that, especially where red
occurred. That night and later, the film
haunted me. I'd be filling a glass with water
or running a bath, and the image of the child
would flood in like a sluice of pain or love
you haven't noticed swelling till the spill.

There's a scene where the father spills
ink or paint over a drawing he's doing. Red
fills the screen. You see at once something about love
and loss is happening. It forms a kind of film
over the celluloid as he runs to raise the child,
already drowned, out of the brown lake water.

Next, the couple in Venice; a maze of water.
Canals, paths confused by mist. Grief spills
over and the father follows a small child
he thinks his because of the hooded coat. Red
of course. They meet a medium with eyes of film.
For comfort, out of foreboding, the couple make love.

Perhaps comfort or foreboding as much as love
held us together in marriage's confluent water.
When years later they showed the film
on TV, I watched the inevitable tragedy spill
onto the screen alone, then opened the door on a red,
hooded coat. It hung, facing me, belonged to our child.

Seeing the red coat dissolved my bones to water.
Hope lies on the surface of love, then spills.
The lost child. That ending. It's all in the film.

Scene on a Hotel Balcony

The wind is fretful, trouble;
snuffs out a light on the balcony,

shorts the electrics. *Listen to it rage,*
says the woman, gripping her arm.

The man looks through the scowling sky.
A red shirt out of nowhere

flies at his face, whips his cheeks,
falls at the woman's feet.

It will be still by morning, he says,
floating his gaze out to sea.

The wind moans in the palms,
hammers and hammers at shutters.

The man smoothes his face. His calm
lashes the woman to silence.

Minutes later, she rises, slams
the balcony door, crosses the room.

The moon is a dazzle at the far window.
It shines like a dangerous freedom.

Forty Years

He looks up
      at the star-stabbed night
            and thinks of their old decision

the pair of them
      sixteen and penniless
            shivering under a barbed-wire sky

the pleasure train
      jolted to a metal-scream stop
            only one track open ahead of them.

Forty years on
      he wishes she'd mention just once
            the life they agreed to renounce.

Poem Withot

Becase I want yo
never again to enter my thoghts
becase I forbid any longing
to pll in your direction
I am writing this poem
withot that certain vowel
the one that says the word *yo*
or wold do if I allowed
the se of that letter –
the one that sonds like yo
when someone names it.
And now I come to think of it
sonds like a female sheep.

From now on girl sheep
are also taboo
and the word *yo*
when it means yo in particlar
will be spoken by me
only on Thrsdays if at all
and only if accompanied by
mltiple crses inslts
or other expressions of disgst
bt never the C word.
And plck ot my eyes
if ever I cry pitifl tears.

You Have Reached Your Destination

And she wouldn't turn back
though the road now
was none too wide,
quiet, not a soul about.

She wouldn't turn back
despite the sign,
Leave your car and go
the rest of the way on foot.

She wouldn't turn back
even at the old stone bridge:
hump-backed, high-sided,
hardly wider than her car.

Rain weighed down the trees.
The track was jumpy
with jagged stone, and by then
she couldn't turn back,

could only manoeuvre round rock
that threatened to bludgeon
the undercarriage. At a closed
farm gate, she stopped.

Beyond was a turning place,
an eccentric old thatch.
She'd come looking for Art:
colour and light, an original.

The gate opened as she pushed.
She was wearing a turban
like Simone de Beauvoir's,
her first drive out since chemo.

The Key

The key is an executive-style five-bedroomed home with open plan living, en-suite bathrooms, a superior range of furnishings

The key is a 6-cylinder elegant, two-door convertible, inspired by high performance yachts, with sporty instrument design and aerodynamically-focused contours

The key is The Silver Cross Surf Aston Martin Edition pram designed to fit the most fast-paced lifestyles. Hand-built with air-ride suspension, forward- and rear-facing pushchair settings, plus a carrycot for the ultimate lie flat environment

The key is an age-defying, wrinkle-reducing facial serum with retinol, vitamins, minerals, lime, kiwi fruit and sweet potato

The key is an 800 calorie a day diet/ a no-carb diet/ a no-fats diet/ a Gwyneth Paltrow quinoa and parsley stalk salad diet/ a no food diet. The key is the Fat is Sexy No Diet Diet

The key is a week's yak trekking in Eastern Mongolia, sleeping in luxury yurts along the way

The key is an exotic pet boa constrictor, a low maintenance pet dragon lizard, an amazing pet baby orang utan

The key is four two-way satellite speakers featuring separate tweeters and woofers for high clarity sound

The key is under the door. I'll be back soon. We can sit and talk. There's bread and cheese in the fridge, a glass of wine if you want it.

Found

From a crowded beach you pick
this one – or this one looks up at you.

One of millions, one alone.
Wave upon wave has moved it

to this shore you walk today.
You turn its smooth weight

in your hand, as it settles and warms.
You notice its form, its shadow and shine,

the briny birth smell of its mystery.
You make a nest in your pocket,

somehow a comfort to think of it there,
your stone. You take it home.

Practising Presence

I'm at the upstairs window,
surveying Suffolk fields, green corn and trees.
I breathe, focus, notice my response.
Practising presence, my book calls this.

The sky of speedwell blue
has speech-bubble clouds. The land, tilted slightly,
sways with May's growth, cow parsley
tall by the grassy banks of the river –

But I'm not looting my mind
to name landscape or weather.
Neither am I entering the usual dream
of being somewhere or somebody else.

No tunes cram my head, no orchestras
crashing, none of those love songs
that yank open doors, exposing the fool
who sobs in the attic, yearning, for years and years.

Practising presence: how hard it is.
Even now I have wandered off to sit writing
at my desk in far off Somerset, a poem
entitled *Practising Presence.*

Acceptance

Here is one of those long French roads
that moves through poplars or poppy fields,
offering a view of mountains perhaps,
or quarries, but which keeps on, unswerving,
refusing to take the high ground or low,
arriving on time, at a place that's new but familiar.

And here is a woman watching
American films, feeding her hunger
with pop corn and sweet chilli crisps.
Here's a middle-aged man returning
from work. He slams shut the door,
cuts short his children, kills the music.

And here is the poet describing all this
with a shrug. Quietly, evenly,
like the moon gracing each cell in the garden
with focused gaze, as though slugs
were as worthy of blessing as doves
or pink-fingered honeysuckle,

as if a man or woman may do almost all
they choose, and still be loved.
Here is the path to acceptance, the lake
that's calm whatever the weather, where
peace-anglers sit, noting what is to be noted,
looking on others, as on themselves,
with the tender, unflinching clarity of the full moon.

Ploubalay

We'd travelled all day,
stopped to camp in Ploubalay,
hungry, throats dry as rust.
A thin street. No cafes.

We came to the one bar:
blank walls, dusty floor,
a man lean as a desert rat,
slumped on a wooden stool.

Pointless to ask, you'd think,
but when we dare to
chance our stuttery French,
Voila! swing doors open

on to a hubbub of tables,
a clatter of cutlery, rising above
a huge hall. A smiling waiter
pulls out a bentwood chair.

Others glide by with platters
of bread, *langoustines, lamb navarin,
tarte aux pommes.* A starched napkin
sits up, pleated with promise.

Sometimes all you need do
is ask, walk through the door
to the next room. Even now,
they are setting a place for you.

Rio, Summer 2014

High on the giant hunchback of the Corcovado,
Christ is a small white cross,
luminous at night.

Even the least religious football fan is touched
by the way he watches over Rio,
arms outstretched.

He's huge up close with soapstone robes, the long
hands of an artist. Lightning
has broken off one finger.

There's a man lying on the ground full stretch,
tubular lens aimed straight up
the Redeemer's nostrils.

A Chinese girl pouts, seducing herself with an iphone.
Everyone smiles, arms spread,
for a selfie with Jesus.

Three musicians explode into samba songs
on the packed down-tram. North,
south, we're all on a high

and a young football supporter from Devon
is wooing an old, gap-toothed Brazilian.
He's down on one knee,

the woman shaking with laughter so that
her belly rocks. Her tee shirt says in English,
Everything in life is for loving.

Mrs Blake Helps Out

That night he retreated to paradise,
again. I was twitchy, itching for something.
It was long after the time I'd stopped noticing
the time. I'd had a glass of wine. Twice.
I tried reading, but no. So I thought I'd surprise
the garden. Even there, silence rushed in
to assault me. I found myself wishing
I had a poet's voice for my inward eyes.

Then I breathed a vision so startling clear
in starlit air that the purple-black night
was suddenly dazzled by arrows of light.
And stuck with a fallow verse, William appeared.
Look Mr Blake! The stars throw down their spears!
I cried. While the tiger burned at our side.

Lilies White Heaven

Lilium Longiflorum

At night, I see them through the window.
White-faced beggars. Or wimpled messengers.
There's longing in the way they stare,
the way they lean towards me, nodding.

They could be from another planet
where everything is made of hurting light.
They seem to want my darkness, the black night
backdrop of my garden, so they can rest.

Or, ambering my arms, they lean, perhaps,
to give; to speak of something, golden-tongued,
some big abstract that I do not understand
in a white language I'm trying to translate.

Iris I

a foetal curl
of stemleafflower
escapes   the papery sheath

reaches
stretches
for light

two blue petals
    unfurl
crowning a night-purple third
daubed with an arc
    of white rays
a golden stripe
in a flick of pizazz
    at its centre

at the line where
petals meet
an opening
    a throat
Come to me come
says the purple tongue

Iris II

I could still see your colours
with eyes shut   blue-violet flare
          a shriek of gold

and the green of you
wet summer leaves climbing spears
          the way you tried to outreach yourself

white rays wild against purple
vanishing
          into a place where
outside becomes inside

I studied the small globe
of your beginnings compacted
          hidden under layers

searched in my twinned self
for the blue dusk to match your blue
          the yellow shout

then it broke in me
nobody else can paint your soul
          or write its name -

each of us guards
          at least one colour
          nobody else can see

Penny Whistle

my little round mouths

    six of them in a row
      open to my dark insides

they want to sing for you

    their high quick whisky jigs
      their slow sad swinnies

they need another mouth
  your mouth your lips
    placed here

your quickened breath
  to blow my music into life

they need your fingers
  here   and here   and here

The Touch

and you came so softly
into the room where I sat
in my reverie
stepping behind me so gently
I didn't know you were there
till your touch on my shoulder
light as a leaf settling

floating up out of my dream
I didn't know who
        our son in Australia
my mother long gone
or a much younger you
who would find me like this
with a touch

hardly daring to

White Water

now that it's over
you think how you gave yourself up
to the man
his orders in Spanish

you stopped thinking you became
your arms working
your feet planted
the roll and ballast of the boat

and the swillicking water
the boat fluming along
drawing closer and closer to white –

till the rush
into sloosh and churn
you no more than a leaf
on the tumblebound swallowdown waters

then it was done

and the wave-smacking bloodwashed glow of it

you gave yourself up to a man
who took you through rapids

you don't even speak Spanish

The Sex Life of Paper Clips

He drew my attention to paper clips,
their furtive encounters, their magic tricks.
How does inanimate stuff like this
secretly manage to shift and hitch?

Necklaces left in a fastened box
end up coiled in unravellable knots
in a ménage à trois with a silver cross
and dangly earrings or bracelet watch.

I'm starting to notice it everywhere:
the toothy kiss of some forks ensnared,
post-tumble tights and a sweater, the pair
in a Velcro clinch on a bedroom chair.

But if it's a crackle of static that smacks
us together, what holds over time is the mass
of poppers and studs, the clasp and the catch.
A hook pulls away and an eye pulls back.

In Need of Some Attention

A big house, double-fronted,
red brick. Wakeful,
restless with creaks
and sighs. A sound
of bone cracks
as we meet the day.

It breathes nicotine,
pipes clogged, so that
some rooms are warm,
some cold as frost.
The hearth too,
bleak, boarded up.

Each metal window frame,
each latch, is arthritic with rust.
The boiler clunks as it pumps,
a heart that won't give up.
A hungry house, this,
energy leaking

through ill-fitting doors,
thin-skinned windows.
A house that's forgotten
bellowing air, the pulse
of music and dance –
too long without children.

The Babysitter Goes Ballroom

It's quiet. He's in a baby sleeping bag,
on his back. Eyes shut, arms raised,
as if to say, *Okay, you win. Game's up.*

At nine o'clock the foot of the bag rises
and flops, while his goldfish mouth
seeks out the taste of Her. A sleepy cry.

Cack-handed strokes, my ministry
of cracked notes only crank the volume up.
Lifted to my shoulder's warmth, he stops –

briefly. Screams. Howls. *Look!* I say. *Look at this!*
We study cardboard books, the orange cat,
a chair; a book of Asian recipes, my coat.

The weather of his screaming soaks
our clothes, stings and lashes me amid
his downpour, whips me to a spinning need

to calm the storm that he's become. Useless
to soothe the rain or tell the wind to settle down
and so I move with it, we dance. We waltz,

we whirl, we wheel as one. Now, silence.
I dare to stop. Then he looks again and knows:
I am not the one. This is not the dance.

After Captain Underpants, the Big Question

'Captain Underpants and the Super Diaper Baby'
is full of poo and crazy dogs and
juice drinks with superpowers.

It's a book well suited
to seven year old boys and this one
tumbles into bed still giggling.

His face shines up from the pillow,
green eyes searching mine.
Gran, do you know the Past?

The soft toys are spellbound, the books
hold their tongues. All there is in that room
is us, in a minute that's deep and long.

Then I say, *Yes, I know the Past.*
I lived there before you were born.
I lived there for a long time.

An Agnostic's Christmas

we travelled for miles
to see the baby
night, day, across continents

carrying clothes for a feverish climate
and presents –
cloth rabbit, musical sheep

where he sleeps
a star turns on a silver string
a gold-winged angel
looks down from the tree

visitors come and go, so many
we all want to see
what the newborn holds
in his waking eyes and feel
            his fingers wrapped around ours

there are men who would skewer a baby

how far would we walk
what jumping seas would we brave
in a loaded boat
to keep him from harm?

his parents bend to him, watchful
his face creased like an ancient's
each sigh a blessing
he stretches his arms and legs

we almost believe
            he will save us

Ferry Across New Year

       they boarded in convoys, on snorting machines,
singly in lorries, rattledown vans, in Beetles and Bubbles,
on foot, on crutches, heaving suitcases, rucksacks, a panting dog

       the bikers in leathers, button-eyed, twizzly-bearded,
perfumed with ale and petrol, tattooed under their hides
with blue mermaids, black devils, snaky skin-graphics

       the leggy girls from Liverpool, long-lashed, lush-lipped
hairtossers, hipswingers, quickwitted teasers and twisters,
minis under maxis, some slant boy on their mezzled minds

       the barlovers, red-cheeked, bow-legged, sloshing
the hard stuff down till the boat's tilting and tossing,
the way to the bog a slalom, the end of it all green faces

       the mothers, shush-shushing, feeding and soothing,
or screeching at their little wailers, their squealing
jack-in-the-box, can't stop, won't stop sparklers

       the siren is booming, the whole caboodle carried away
on the waves, none of them knowing come this time next year,
who will be famous or ruined, who will be lost or saved.

Washing the Buddha

In heat, wind, downpour, knee-high snow,
he sat on.

When kids pelted his head with soil and stones,
he sat on.

Juddering in the removal van's closed dark,
and rehoused

in the seeping corner where midges dance at dusk,
he sat on.

I wander unfamiliar paths, turn and turn again,
while he sits on.

And when I scrub the mildewed spots from his
crossed legs,

he sits on. Patiently he sits, as I scrape away
the yellow moss

and bathe his crown, face, chest, his mottled
arms and back.

I tip him sideways, backwards, upside down.
Gently though,

and when the green scum froths, I sluice it off
till he is clean again.

And then we sit together, me and Buddha.
We sit on.

Indigo Dreams Publishing Ltd
24, Forest Houses
Cookworthy Moor
Halwill
Beaworthy
Devon
EX21 5UU
www.indigodreams.co.uk